MILNER CRAFT SERIES

Embroidered Garden Flowers

BY DIANA LAMPE
WITH JANE FISK

SALLY MILNER PUBLISHING

First published in 1994 by
Sally Milner Publishing Pty Ltd
at 'The Pines'
RMMB 54 Burra Road
Burra Creek NSW 2620
Australia

Reprinted 1991, 1992, 1993 (twice), 1994 (twice), 1995 (twice), 1996, 1997

© Embroidery design and artwork, Diana Lampe 1991
© Text Jane Fisk 1991
© Text in Flower and Stitch Glossary, Diana Lampe 1991

Design by Gatya Kelly, Doric Order
Photography by Andre Martin
Stitch illustrations by Don Bradford
Flower illustrations by Diana Lampe
Typeset in Australia by Asset Typesetting Pty Ltd
Printed in Australia by Impact Printing, Melbourne

National Library of Australia
Cataloguing-in-Publication data:

Lampe, Diana.
    Embroidered garden flowers

    ISBN 1 86351 043 5.

    1.Embroidery — Patterns. 2. Decoration and ornament
    —Plant forms. I. Fisk, Jane II. Title.

746.44041

To my father – a man of great integrity.
We shared a precious gift – a fascination with, and a love of, nature.

Oscar Frederick Lampe
29 July 1911–11 July 1990
'Nebea', Coonamble, NSW

Diana Lampe, 1991

ACKNOWLEDGEMENTS

W e wish to thank Dollfus-Mieg & Cie – Paris, for granting permission to use the DMC© trademark throughout this book.

JOINT ACKNOWLEDGEMENT

Affinity Plus Creative Needlework is a shop in Canberra founded and run by Paddy and Jack Hornsby. We are among a number of needleworkers who conduct classes at their premises.

Paddy and Jack and their staff have created a warm and friendly atmosphere in their shop, making it a pleasure for both teachers and students. We take this opportunity to thank them both for their enthusiasm and support in developing and extending Diana's repertoire and in encouraging the realisation of this book. We thank them also for the many happy hours we have spent at Affinity Plus.

Diana Lampe and Jane Fisk, 1991

ACKNOWLEDGEMENTS BY DIANA LAMPE

The pleasure and joy I have felt in writing this book would never have eventuated but for the untiring patience and encouragement of my family. To my husband, David Harper, and our children, Charlotte, Sophie and Nicholas, my love and deep gratitude – and also to my mother, May Lampe, who encouraged me to experiment and develop my needlework skills from the time I first picked up a needle and thread at the age of three.

My sincere thanks to Jane and Freddy Fisk for the realisation of a dream: to Jane for her faith in me and my embroidery and her devotion to the task of writing; and to Freddy for the benefit of his wealth of experience and for the many hours spent at his computer typing and developing our text.

Many close friends and students have influenced this book with their enthusiasm and encouragement. My sincere thanks to them for their support. In particular I would like to thank Roslyn Hodgkins who inspired me to start embroidering flowers and gardens.

Special thanks are due to John Dwyer and Bryanne Barnett without whose caring support I would not have had the confidence and perseverance to embark on and complete the task, and to Carmen Garcia, who has cared for my family for many years.

Finally my appreciation to Sally Milner, our publisher, for seeing the potential of my embroidery, to Marg Bowman, who worked closely with us bringing the book together, and Don Bradford for his excellent stitch illustrations. Thanks also to Ross Henty, for his clear and helpful notes on the framing of needlework, and to Geoffrey Brooks and Gillian Falvey for their constructive criticism of the descriptions and instructions and their help with the preparation of the manuscript.

Diana Lampe, 1991

ACKNOWLEDGEMENTS BY JANE FISK

My sincere thanks to Diana for giving me the opportunity to play a part in bringing her unique talent to all who love embroidery.

Appreciation goes to many people but in particular to the following:

My husband, Freddy, for his encouragement, untiring assistance and firm belief I could write this book; my son, Peter, my daughter-in-law, Jenny, and my daughter, Rosemary, for expressing their pleasure in receiving my embroideries as gifts; Dr T. G. Lithgow and Robyn Brown whose skill, care and understanding enabled me to continue with my embroidery; Barbara Orchard for her interest and helpful reading of the text, and finally, but most importantly, my friends and students who showed their enthusiasm by asking almost weekly when the book would be published.

Jane Fisk, 1991

I should like to make it quite clear that the text of this book is simply a description of Diana's work. The methods described, the selection of stitches and colours used, the designs, and the general approach, are all Diana's. Only the words are mine.

My role in writing this text has been that of a student reporting the teaching of a great artist in what might be described as a Master Class in embroidery. It is my hope that I have been able to do this in a simple and straightforward way that will enable a great number of ordinary people like myself, whether experienced embroiderers or beginners, to share the lasting benefits and delights that we, who have attended Diana's classes, have gained from them.

Jane Fisk, 1991

CONTENTS

PREFACE

Brush up on your basic embroidery stitches in the most delightful way.
A standard rose, an agapanthus and a violet one day; a foxglove or a
hollyhock the next.

Two days, 10am-3pm

This description, which appeared in the Affinity Plus Creative Needlework program for one of the many classes held in Canberra for the first half of 1988, was irresistible – I enrolled in the class. The Cottage Garden, completed and framed, had to be followed by the Summer Garland, then the Spring Garden. And so my love for this delightful embroidery grew.

Diana, with her talent for embroidery and her love of gardens, has re-created the flowers which bloom in her garden, using a few basic stitches. Realistic colour is a most important part of her designs and she has chosen with care and skill to ensure that the colours are as close to nature as possible. To achieve this, flowers were freshly picked from her own garden and matched with a full range of DMC stranded cotton.

From the time Diana discovered that basic embroidery stitches and natural colours could be used to realistic effect in the depiction of flowers, she spent many years perfecting her unique talent. Only when the flower was lifelike was she satisfied. Many trials and changes were involved before the perfect method of working was arrived at and a totally realistic, identifiable, flower 'bloomed' on fabric.

It was obvious a book of special quality was needed to describe her techniques: one where the readers, once captivated with the colours and settings of the gardens, would feel inspired and confident enough to embroider one themselves. And, ultimately, they would have the expertise to create a design of their own.

A book that was self-contained and uncomplicated was the objective. It should be enjoyable reading, yet provide the fundamentals of embroidery required to produce a good result. These, then, were our aims in creating this book – aims we hope have been fully realised.

Flowers are some of nature's most beautiful creations and in the embroidered gardens featured in the following pages, their colours are long-lasting, and their fragrance can easily be imagined.

INTRODUCTION

Over the past few years, there has been a revival of the gentle arts, of which embroidery is just one branch. This book is intended to contribute to this revival by bringing specialised needlework once more to the forefront.

Flower embroidery has long had great appeal. Diana Lampe's work in this field has introduced a degree of realism by its adherence to the correct use of colour and by its emphasis on placing the flowers in their natural setting – in a garden.

Instructions in this book have been kept simple and direct to ensure that neither beginners nor experienced needleworkers will have any difficulty in finding their way around. None need feel that the embroidery is beyond them.

The book opens with a section on how to get started. This includes some notes on the basic materials and equipment you will need. This is followed by a short discussion about design and the way your project can be finished and presented.

The flower glossary gives clear instructions for each species and includes the method of working, the DMC stranded cotton numbers for the colours used, and details of the needles required. This information, combined with the sample embroidery and drawing of each flower, should make it possible even for the inexperienced needleworker to begin a project, large or small, without hesitation.

We have also included a glossary covering the basic stitches used, to cater for those who have little or no prior knowledge of embroidery techniques. Please take the time to read this glossary. Even experienced embroiderers may find some useful suggestions that will help with working some of the stitches.

We have included colour plates of a few smaller items which feature some of the embroidery described. These articles make delightful gifts and are less time-consuming to complete than the larger projects, as well as being excellent practice pieces. It is a fact that the more you do, the greater the ease of working, and the more accomplished you will become.

The Appendices list the prerequisites for working the Cottage Garden, the Spring Garden and the Spring Garland. A complete list of colour thread numbers for each of these designs is given, simplifying the purchase of what you need.

Once you have embarked on your first project, we are sure you will join the ever-increasing numbers who wish there were more hours in the day in which to indulge their new-found enjoyment. Take heart. You will make time somehow – we all do.

We hope you will derive great pleasure from this book and that you will enjoy the feeling of achievement upon completing your first project.

GETTING STARTED

The kiss of the sun for pardon,
The song of the birds for mirth,
One is nearer God's Heart in a garden
Than anywhere else on earth.

God's Garden
Dorothy Frances Gurney (1858–1932)

In preparing to embroider your garden, first decide upon a basic design. It may be one copied from this book or a design of your own. Should you feel confident in creating your own, planning it on paper first will give an indication of the finished size. This is an important consideration when cutting your fabric.

With experience, your embroidered garden may 'bloom' straight from the needle – without planning – evolving rather as gardens do in nature.

The measurements given for the gardens in this book are of the embroidered work to the edge of the picture mount. This is the area actually seen when the work is framed. Allow generous fabric borders of at least 10-12 centimetres (4-5 inches) beyond this on all sides to enable the framer to stretch and mount the finished work easily.

Having decided upon the scale of the design, you may care to overlock the edges of the fabric to prevent fraying. Sew a tacking thread to indicate the approximate size of the embroidered work, centring it on your fabric. Should your completed garden be slightly larger than originally contemplated, you will not find this a problem if you have allowed generous borders.

As these gardens depend heavily upon natural colour, do not spoil your work by using colours that are 'near enough'. The colours given here have been matched to the flowers with considerable care. Check in the flower glossary that you have the correct thread colours for the flowers to 'bloom' effectively in your garden.

Naturally, flowers come in an endless variety of colours and tonings. It has not been possible to list all of these in this book. Feel free to experiment by matching other colours with fresh flowers and leaves, or by working from a photograph.

In a short time, you will become more observant and find yourself studying flower compositions in detail. You will look automatically to see if the leaves are in pairs, and take care to count how many petals form each flower. Flowers will be seen in a new light – they *can* be embroidered using a suitable stitch and the truest colour possible.

Make your whole method of working as efficient as possible. It is helpful to keep all the threads for each flower together, either in a small, labelled, plastic bag or wound on a card and marked with the appropriate thread number. When the band with the thread number has been lost, it is difficult to guess where the thread belongs. Initial care with labelling will avoid this problem.

You are now ready to start. Choose an agreeable place, in the garden or indoors. With a comfortable chair, good light, your necessities on a table at your side, and beautiful music playing, you will gain considerable pleasure from creating your embroidered garden.

CHAPTER 2

NECESSITIES

FABRIC

Natural-coloured fabric gives the most pleasing effect and allows the beauty and lustre of the thread colours to be shown to their best advantage. Fine Irish linen, natural or seeded homespun, silk and calico are ideal. These are washable after the embroidery is completed. Irish linen has been used for the illustrations of the Cottage Garden, Spring Garden, Spring Garland and Initials.

THREADS

DMC stranded cotton is used throughout. The number of strands required varies from flower to flower. The colours have been blended in some flowers to obtain the truest tonings possible. Wisteria, Daphne, magnolia, French lavender and agapanthus are examples where this has been done.

NEEDLES

Embroidery crewel needles Nos 7, 8, and 9 are used for the embroidery in this book, with the exception of bullion stitch for which straw or millinery needles Nos 8 and 9 are required. Further information is given in Sewing Notes.

EMBROIDERY SCISSORS

Embroidery scissors come in all shapes and sizes but are generally small with long, sharp blades tapering to a point to allow for easy unpicking should this be necessary. The traditional gold-plated, stork-shaped scissors are aesthetically pleasing and comfortable to use.

PINCUSHION

A pincushion is handy for holding needles when using a variety of colours for embroidering a particular flower.

PENCILS FOR MARKING

A soft lead pencil is all that is required for marking the fabric for placement of designs. It will wash out when the embroidery is completed.

EMBROIDERY HOOPS

Embroidery hoops are available in a range of sizes from most needlework and craft shops. Whether you use these or not is a matter of personal preference. More details are given in Sewing Notes.

SEWING BASKET

An attractive sewing basket or box containing all your accessories will keep everything close to hand and make your work more enjoyable whenever you have the spare time to embroider your garden.

CHAPTER 3

DESIGN

The design can be directly copied, perhaps from a picture or a drawing, or adapted to suit your own taste. In class, it was interesting to note how the completed gardens, all taken from the one design, differed slightly one from the other: some a little larger or smaller; more blooms on a bush; extra flowers added or some left out. This was pleasing as the embroidery in the classes and this book is done free-hand and not on a traditional pre-stamped cloth, therefore allowing for individuality of interpretation. However, because the set colours for the flowers were adhered to, the overall effect was similar.

A Cottage Garden and a Spring Garden have been chosen for inclusion in this book. Some flowers overlap from one season to the next. There are also many other flowers that could 'bloom' in these gardens, their colours and tonings carefully blended to create a pleasing balance.

If you wish, choose your favourite flowers and embroider them together in your own combination. Feel free to use artistic licence. The possibilities are limited only by your imagination.

To add a touch of realism, some of your gardens can be invaded by a few of the gardener's pests and friends: a snail with a silvery trail, a spider spinning a silken web between flowers, and a butterfly.

A bird bath under a tree, a sundial surrounded by flowers, or a garden seat in front of an herbaceous border could all be added to create focal points in other designs.

Perhaps there is a corner in your own garden which gives you particular enjoyment; capture it on film so that when the flowers fade and the season changes, you will have a photograph from which to work.

PROPORTION

While it is virtually impossible to show all flowers to scale, it is not difficult to indicate an obvious difference in size. Violets and forget-me-nots, for example, being so much smaller than hollyhocks and foxgloves, can be tucked in between larger flowers, giving the impression of delicacy. Further balance of scale can be achieved by the placement of taller and larger flowers in the background and by working forward to the smaller and more delicate flowers in the foreground.

Added pleasure from your finished embroidery will be derived when someone readily identifies the flowers you have worked. This will largely depend on your using the correct colours and keeping large and small flowers in relative proportion. If your scale does vary a little, don't despair; it is the overall balance between colour and texture within the embroidery that will make your garden 'bloom'.

CHAPTER 4

FINISHING AND FRAMING

The placement of your signature and the date gives the finishing touch to your embroidered garden.

Museum and private conservators have recognised and highlighted the importance of this means of identification for large and small works of art: surely, your embroidered garden, after all the hours of work you have put into it, will qualify as one of these?

Extreme care is needed when washing your completed embroidery. Reaching this stage is most exciting. At this point, all those hours of work are about to be rewarded by the finished work appearing in all its beauty, making the whole project worthwhile.

Wash the embroidery in warm water using pure soap and rinse it very thoroughly in distilled water to remove any chemical traces present in the washing water. Do not wring the fabric as this would cause creasing that would be difficult to remove. Either shake out the excess water, or allow it to drip.

Correct pressing is most important. Lay the *wet* embroidery right side down between two layers of dye-free fabric (a white linen tea-towel is ideal) and place it on a folded towel. Press with a hot iron. The layers of fabric will prevent scorching of the embroidery and eliminate any indentations the towel may cause. Pressing this way will not flatten the embroidery: it will actually raise it, bringing your garden to life.

The frame and mount are a matter of individual taste. Should the picture be hung in a room where there is an open fire, glass will keep it smoke-free. The glass should not be in contact with the embroidery as it could be crushed. To prevent this, a double mount is sometimes required. Plexiglas reduces the penetration of ultra-violet rays and helps to prevent fading, but it is easily scratched. Avoid hanging your embroidery in direct sunlight as the colours will almost certainly fade.

We have included in Appendix E some notes on framing and conservation of needlework by Ross Henty from the Canberra Art Framing Company. Discuss these notes with your own framer to ensure that the correct materials are used. With a professional framer you will feel secure in the knowledge that your embroidery will remain in good condition for years to come and will be treasured by future generations.

CHAPTER 5

SEWING NOTES

We both enjoy teaching, finding it rewarding and satisfying to share knowledge and skills. A whole day's teaching can be made magic by seeing the delight on people's faces when an apparent difficulty is removed by a small suggestion, or when students first understand the reason behind a particular method of working. The atmosphere in our classes is relaxed. Throughout, we discuss sewing techniques and materials, as well as pleasant incidents of our daily lives.

We thought we would share some of the more practical things we discuss in the hope that you, too, will find them helpful.

One of the great mysteries of sewing seems to surround the uses of different types of needles, particularly in embroidery. The names by which some needles are known are self-explanatory: for example, tapestry, chenille and beading needles. Embroidery crewel needles and straw or millinery needles are used for the embroidery in this book.

Needles come in a range of sizes, and the sizes relate to the thickness of the shafts. An easy way of remembering sizes is to relate them to knitting needles: the size with the highest number is the finest, and the lowest number is the thickest.

Embroidery crewel needles range in size from 3 to 10. The finest needles are used for one strand of embroidery thread; the largest for six strands. The eye of the needle varies in size to accommodate the number of strands.

The shaft of these needles is a comfortable length for most embroidery.

The embroidery in this book requires the use of size 7, 8 and 9 embroidery crewel needles. These are available in individual packets each containing needles of one size. Some flowers, such as foxgloves, are worked in various shades and it is advisable to have several needles of the same size to hand. The flower glossary indicates the size of the needle required and the number of strands appropriate for each of these sizes.

Straw or millinery needles are best used for bullion stitch. The shaft of these needles is the same thickness from the eye to where it begins tapering to the point. This allows the wraps of thread to slide easily off the needle. The shaft of these needles ranges from a thick No 3 for six strands, to a fine No 10 for one strand. To accommodate the many wraps of thread needed for long stretches of bullion stitch, as in the branches of the Daphne bush, these needles have a longer shaft than most others.

People who find bullion stitch difficult, or have obtained unsatisfactory results, are often using an embroidery crewel needle. The eye of these needles is thicker than the shaft, making it difficult for the wraps of thread to slide off easily, resulting in uneven and often lumpy bullions. The use of a straw needle will overcome this problem.

DMC stranded cotton is sold in skeins 8 metres (approximately 9 yards) in length held by paper bands at either end. One of these bands has clear instructions on how to remove the thread without tangling; an important consideration when winding the thread on to cards or removing just a short length. It is desirable to thread your needle with the end indicated in the instructions so that you are sewing with the twist of the thread, allowing it to glide through the fabric. When winding thread on to cards, start with the opposite end; in this way, you will always thread your needle in the correct direction.

Threads should be cut into lengths of no more than 40 centimetres (16 inches). This is approximately the distance from the tip of the index finger to the elbow. As the thread passes through the fabric many times it tends to wear and become thin. It really is worth making the effort to re-thread your needle several times rather than be tempted to use a long thread which will result in poor quality work.

To allow the natural lustre of the thread to shine through, the individual strands should be carefully parted before working. To do this, hold the thread (cut to the suggested length) between the thumb and forefinger and pull each strand directly upwards. This method will not only prevent the strands becoming tangled but will also protect the fine fibres from damage. Place the required number of strands together again – whether it be two or six strands.

Needles with small eyes are often difficult to thread but, with the aid of a metal needle threader, this can be overcome. For easy threading of a needle with multiple strands, cut the ends of the thread on a slant.

We have mentioned the need to keep the threads together for each flower to facilitate the use of the correct colours. Needlework and craft shops have a wide range of products suitable for this purpose. For example, there are plastic boxes with compartments and cards and there are folders for holding lengths of thread in neat order with card indexes for the thread numbers. Such systems are very useful and eliminate time-consuming and frustrating searches.

Some people find they work better with an embroidery hoop, while others find using one awkward. This is a matter of personal choice, but a hoop is invaluable for working French knots where the fabric needs to be kept taut. Delphiniums, with their myriad of French knots, are worked more easily using a hoop.

Do not be tempted to run threads more than 5 millimetres (about ¼ inch) from one flower to another as they often show through the fabric once it has been washed and pressed, thus spoiling your work. To prevent any underlying threads from showing through, flowers such as foxgloves should be worked down the stems. Do not jump from one stem to another. On the other hand, it is more convenient to work the centres of shasta daisies, for example, from one to another as the petals will be worked over these underlying threads.

Avoid leaving a needle in your embroidery for a lengthy period. It would be such a pity to find it had rusted and left a mark in your fabric. Should you not be able to continue with your embroidery for a few days, roll it on to the cardboard cylinder from a roll of paper towels. This will prevent creases developing which can be difficult to remove.

Once your embroidered work has been washed and pressed, hold it up to the light and check there are no small tags left at the end of knots which might have been pushed into an unembroidered area and so show through. You will be satisfied with your framed work if you have attended to these small but telling details.

CHAPTER 6

COTTAGE GARDEN

Soon we shall have gold-dusted snapdragon,
Sweet William with his lovely cottage-smell,
And stocks in fragrant blow.

Matthew Arnold (1822–1888)

Banks of brightly coloured and fragrant flowers are the essence of a cottage garden. These pleasing gardens, bringing a sense of nostalgia for a bygone era, are gaining in popularity. Diana has created a small Cottage Garden design massed with well-known and best-loved flowers. Among them, tall hollyhocks, a stately standard rose, magnificent agapanthus and fragrant French lavender are delightfully combined with delicate English primroses, violets and forget-me-nots.

Before commencing work on your garden, read again carefully the chapter on getting started to ensure that you have allowed sufficient fabric for your garden, taking into consideration any extensions or modifications you intend to introduce.

Should you decide to copy the cottage garden illustrated, the photograph will be a guide to the order in which the flowers should be placed. The actual size of the garden illustrated is 270 mm (10½″) wide and 100 mm (4″) high.

A tacking-thread outline of the finished work should be centred on the fabric. To help keep your garden baseline even, lightly draw a straight line approximately 2 centimetres (1 inch) from the bottom tacking line. You can, of course, work slightly below this line with some flowers in order to give the garden a natural look.

The larger background flowers, the standard rose, agapanthus, hollyhocks and foxgloves are worked first. A pencil mark for each of these will help with their placement and will ensure that sufficient space is allowed for the larger foreground flowers of periwinkle, French lavender and shasta daisies.

Delphiniums in their different shades of blue can be worked behind other foreground flowers, thus considerably reducing your working time – they are very time-consuming. This can also be done with the foxgloves, if you wish.

Delicate sprays of gypsophila (baby's breath) can be tucked behind and in between the foliage. A few stems of French lavender worked behind foreground flowers give a little extra colour if needed. Forget-me-nots, violets, English primroses, cyclamen, heart's-ease, cottage pinks and alyssum can now be worked in and around the stems of the other plants.

Finally, find a suitable place to work a silken web for your spider and an appropriate space for your signature and date.

Refer to Appendix A for a list of all the colour numbers of the DMC stranded cotton, the needle types and sizes, and the fabric you will need to embroider this garden.

CHAPTER 7

SPRING GARDEN

Buttercups and daisies,
Oh, the pretty flowers;
Coming ere the springtime,
To tell of sunny hours.

Buttercups and Daisies
Mary Howitt (1799–1888)

Spring, one of the loveliest seasons, has been fully captured in this beautiful Spring Garden design. Wisteria covering a pergola, nodding daffodils, scented Daphne, Dutch hyacinths and tiny violets are just a few of the many flowers featured in this embroidery.

Carefully read again the chapter on getting started and follow the guidelines given for the Cottage Garden.

Start by embroidering the pergola, the heavy trunk of the wisteria vine and the smaller branches. Heavily cover these with flowers, scattering leaves throughout. Some flowers and leaves will be placed over parts of the already embroidered pergola.

The magnolia tree and Daphne bush can then be embroidered; be sure to leave sufficient space for the smaller flowers below. The flowers in the foreground such as snowflakes, daffodils, Dutch hyacinths, Winter rose *(Helleborus)*, flowering almond cherry *(Prunus)*, English bluebells and Solomon's seal can then be worked. French lavender and periwinkle can be tucked behind the larger flowers.

Spaces around and below can now be filled with the smaller flowers – forget-me-nots, cyclamen, English primroses, violets, grape hyacinths and lily-of-the-valley.

The flagstones, cat and snail are the final touches to your Spring Garden. Don't forget your signature and the date.

Refer to Appendix B for a list of all the colour numbers of the DMC stranded cotton, the needle types and sizes, and the fabric you will need to embroider this garden. The actual size of this garden is 270 mm wide and 125 mm (10½″ x 4¾″) high.

SPRING GARLAND

This small embroidery is one of Diana's prettiest and most delicate. She has chosen flowers from her Spring Garden design, blending their colours into a verdant, subtly hued garland. Tiny violets, pink forget-me-nots, English primroses and spikes of French lavender peek from behind the beautiful racemes of wisteria, splendid magnolia flowers and branches of forsythia blossoms.

The amount of fabric required for this work will largely depend on the size of the garland you propose and how you wish it to be framed. Diana's garland is 130 mm (5¼″) in diameter.

Lightly mark a circle on the fabric and divide it into thirds to give an even balance of flowers. If your garland is to be larger than that illustrated, it would be advisable to divide it into fifths.

Sew a tacking thread, using one strand of pale green, on the pencil line as a guide should your outline fade. Your embroidery will cover and hide this thread.

The larger flowers, magnolia, wisteria and Daphne, should be worked first. Distribute them evenly in the marked segments. Branches of forsythia and groups of Winter rose (*helleborus*) follow with the smaller flowers – English primroses, violets, blue and pink forget-me-nots, periwinkle and French lavender heads. A touch of white has been introduced into the garland with a few cyclamen and tiny sprays of lily-of-the-valley. A dainty butterfly and your initials and date will complete this charming piece.

Refer to Appendix C for a list of all the colour numbers of the DMC stranded cotton, the needle types and sizes, and the fabric you will need to embroider this work.

COTTAGE GARDEN

Spring

SPRING GARDEN

SPRING GARLAND

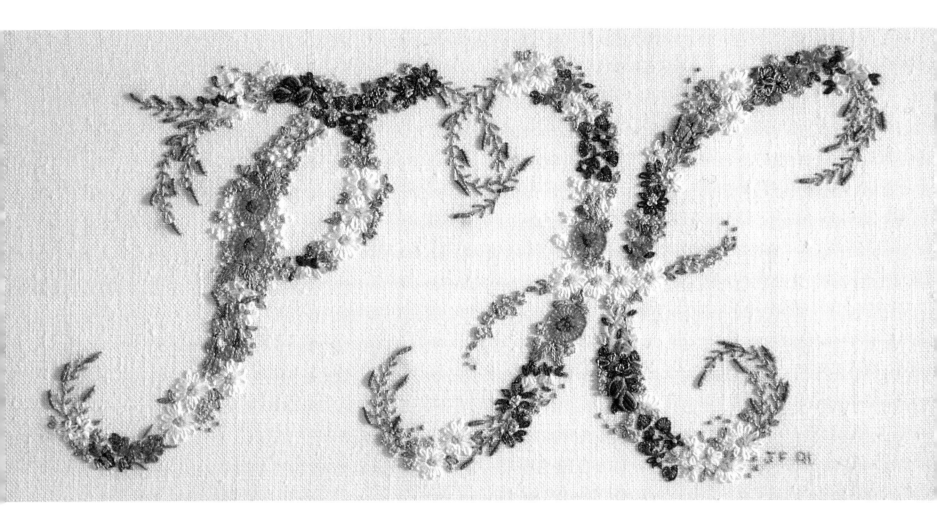

EMBROIDERED INITIALS

GIFT IDEAS

FLOWER SAMPLER

FLOWER SAMPLER

Key to Cottage Garden

1 Agapanthus
2 Alyssum
3 Cottage Pinks
4 Cyclamen
5 Delphinium
6 English Primrose
7 Forget-me-nots
8 Foxglove

9 French Lavender
10 Gypsophila
11 Hearts-ease
12 Hollyhock
13 Periwinkle
14 Rose
15 Shasta Daisy
16 Violet

NOT ACTUAL SIZE

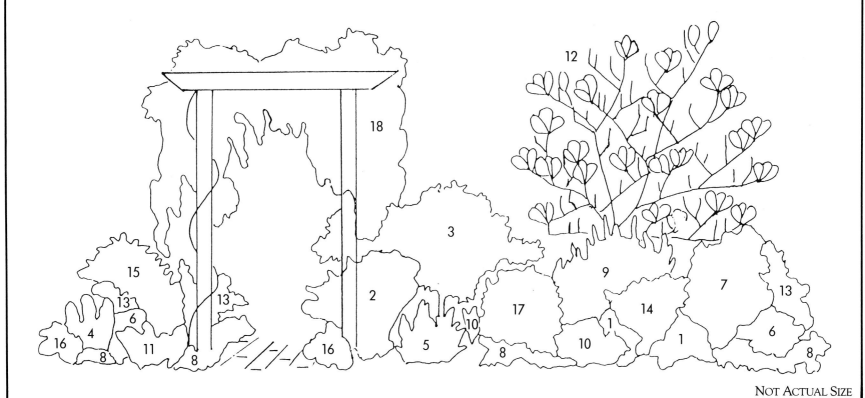

Key to Spring Garden

1 Cyclamen
2 Daffodil
3 Daphne
4 Dutch Hyacinth
5 English Bluebell
6 English Primrose
7 Flowering Almond Cherry
8 Forget-me-nots
9 French Lavender

10 Grape Hyacinth
11 Lily-of-the-valley
12 Magnolia
13 Periwinkle
14 Snowflake
15 Solomon's Seal
16 Violet
17 Winter Rose
18 Wisteria

NOT ACTUAL SIZE

Key to Flower Samplers

1 Agapanthus
2 Alyssum
3 Cottage Pinks
4 Cyclamen
5 Daffodil
6 Daphne
7 Delphinium

8 Dutch Hyacinth
9 English Bluebell
10 English Primrose
11 Flowering Almond Cherry
12 Forget-me-not
13 Forsythia
14 Foxglove

15 French Lavender
16 Grape Hyacinth
17 Gypsophila
18 Heart's-ease
19 Hollyhock
20 Lily-of-the-valley
21 Magnolia
22 Periwinkle

23 Rose
24 Shasta Daisy
25 Snowflake
26 Solomon's Seal
27 Violet
28 Winter Rose
29 Wisteria

Key to Embroidered Gifts

1 Pincushion by Lois Kinsman
2 Pincushion by Chris Bromfield
3 Sewing baskets by Jane Fisk
4 Embroidered pullover by Diana Lampe
5 Cushion by Jane Fisk
6 Cushion by Maggie Taylor
7 Coathanger by Diana Lampe
8 Wickerwork basket by Jane Fisk
9 Lavender sachet by Jane Fisk
10 Towel by Jane Fisk
11 Brooch by Diana Lampe
12 Handkerchiefs by Jane Fisk

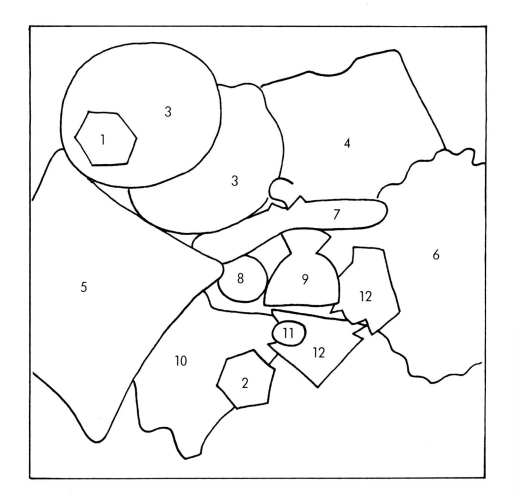

CHAPTER 9

EMBROIDERED INITIALS

Diana's daughter, Sophie, was the inspiration behind the embroidered initials. Having seen her mother working flowers into a garland, she requested her own initial be worked in the same way.

Embroidered initials make excellent personalised gifts. They can be used in many ways: as a framed picture or as the cover of a special book or album. On a smaller scale, two or more initials look delightful worked on the top of a very special sewing box.

Many books contain outlines of monograms or initials that are suitable for flower embroidery. One book in particular, *A Garden Alphabet* by John Harris (Octopus Books) has an alphabet of flower initials of pleasing proportions and flowing lines. If this book is not available in your bookshop, your local library may be able to get it for you. We have included two alphabets in our book which you can use for framed embroideries and other pieces. The letters can be enlarged depending on the size you choose to work.

Begin by tracing your chosen initial in a heavy outline on transparent paper; put your fabric, cut to generous proportions, over the paper and place them both over a light-box.

A light-box can be improvised by shining a bedside lamp under a glass-topped table or a sheet of glass placed on two pillars of books.

Re-trace the initial on to the fabric with a soft lead pencil. Run a fine tacking thread (using one strand of a pale shade of green) over the outline. Should your pencil outline fade during working, your thread will be a guide, and will be covered subsequently by the embroidered work.

With the exception of the French lavender stems, only flower heads and leaves have been worked in the initial illustrated. A pleasing balance is obtained by grouping larger flower heads such as hollyhocks or agapanthus on the long axis of the letter, graduating to smaller flowers at the ends. French lavender is ideal for the end of an initial as the stems will fan to create a fern-like effect. Additional leaves and French knots will achieve a soft, flowing line.

Colour balance is important, but, as there are many flowers from which to choose, this should not be a problem. Should an area appear a little subdued, small flower heads such as forget-me-nots, English primroses or violets can be tucked in to add more colour.

CHAPTER 10

GIFT IDEAS

There is an art in giving. For most occasions, a handmade gift is received with pleasure. Perhaps it is the appreciation of the many hours of work involved or the very personal nature of the gift, for often the person giving gains as much pleasure as the recipient. Framed embroidered gardens are wonderful wedding gifts and lasting treasures.

In classes for Diana's embroidered gardens many of the students use their imagination in applying the techniques learned to a number of different projects, many of them suitable gift items.

Of the wealth of articles created, who could resist pastel-pink quilted toddler's overalls, the bib embellished with hollyhocks, shasta daisies and forget-me-nots; or baby singlets sprinkled with the simplest of flowers or more sophisticated sprays of lavender? Small felt teddy bears with delicate flowers embroidered across their fat tummies were particularly engaging, and a pair of piqué baby shoes tied with silk ribbons and adorned with clusters of forget-me-nots on their tiny toes enchanted us all. A fabric sewing box, the lid embroidered with a garden, was, we were told to our amazement, regularly popped into the washing-machine. There was a paperweight enclosing a miniature garden embroidered on white pure silk, intended for a special birthday gift.

All of these could be pleasing gifts, and all incorporate a small selection of Diana's flower embroidery. We have included a colour plate of a few items that you may be tempted to make. A key to these items can be found accompanying the colour section. Hopefully, they will encourage you to develop your own ideas.

EMBROIDERED PULLOVER

One of Diana's pullovers is always admired whenever she wears it. Using a large tapestry needle and DMC tapestry wool, she embroidered a store purchased Shetland pullover with some simplified versions of her garden flowers. When working on loosely woven fabrics such as this, care needs to be taken not to pull the embroidery thread too tightly.

SEWING BASKETS

Many natural-cane baskets, spray-painted in pastel colours, lend themselves perfectly to sewing baskets. They look particularly attractive with the added interest of an embroidered padded base or lid.

HANDKERCHIEFS

Linen handkerchiefs are useful for putting inside Christmas and birthday cards, and are always acceptable gifts. They become something special when the corners are embroidered with fine sprays of lavender, circles of forget-me-nots or small bouquets of mixed flowers.

CUSHIONS

We all love the luxury of beautiful down-filled cushions. They make lovely gifts when matched to the decor of a room. One of those illustrated is made with moiré taffeta and embellished with a circle of Diana's flowers. It is embroidered in six strands of thread, using a No 3 straw or millinery needle. The bow is worked in satin stitch.

Scrumptious is the only word to describe the other small cushion. Flowers have been embroidered on off-white silk and surrounded by a froth of lace.

TOWELS

Guest towels made from towelling are a practical gift, but, when embroidered their appearance is considerably enhanced. For ease of working, choose towels with a heavy woven band across the bottom. Six strands of thread are used with a No 3 straw or millinery needle. A matching set comprising bath towel, hand towel and face-washer for the guest bathroom makes an appropriate engagement present.

LAVENDER SACHETS

Little embroidered sachets filled with lavender or pot-pourri and tied with ribbons are always welcome. A variety of fabrics can be used.

COATHANGERS

These are luxury gifts. The one illustrated has been embroidered on homespun fabric with a small, finely worked garden.

PINCUSHIONS

Embroiderers need pincushions but not all can boast lovely hexagonal ones embroidered in the centre. Fill them firmly with toy wadding. If you feel they are too special merely for pins, use them on a dressing-table to hold brooches.

BROOCHES

Small silver and gold brooches suitable for insertion of embroidery can be purchased at most needlework and craft shops.

CHAPTER 11

FLOWER GLOSSARY

This glossary gives the colour thread numbers and the method of working for the individual flowers and foliage in this book.

Before commencing work, carefully read the details for each flower, relating the text to the drawing and the embroidered illustration. Remember that the embroidered illustration will help you create the correct sense of scale.

Many flowers, such as forget-me-nots, English primroses and periwinkle, have five petals. To space these petals evenly, imagine a 'stick figure' with a head, two arms and two legs; these positions will help with placement.

For the flowers worked in buttonhole stitch – daffodils, English bluebells, foxgloves, heart's-ease and hollyhocks – it is necessary to begin working this stitch from the outside edge. Please refer to the stitch glossary and the illustrations of the flowers.

Many of the flower stems and branches are worked in couching. This is a quick and easy stitch, but it is advisable to work with two needles and to keep them on top of your work to prevent tangling. Two strands of thread are laid down and couched into position with one strand throughout.

All French knots in this glossary are worked with only one twist unless otherwise stated, as in the case of hollyhocks and foxgloves.

LEFT-HANDED EMBROIDERERS

If you are left-handed, you will find the following suggestions helpful.

- When working buttonhole stitch, you will find it easier to work from right to left.
- Hollyhock flowers will be more easily worked in a clockwise direction.
- For foxgloves and English bluebells, work from the right-hand side across the stem to the left.
- For circular flowers such as agapanthus, try working anti-clockwise.

NEEDLES

Embroidery crewel needles are used for all stitches except bullion stitch, for which a straw or millinery needle is required.

Needles for the individual flowers vary in accordance with the stitch used and the number of strands required. Guidelines are as follows:

- No 7 embroidery crewel needles for three to four strands of thread.
- No 8 embroidery crewel needles for two strands of thread.
- No 8 straw or millinery needles for two strands of thread.
- No 9 embroidery crewel needles for one strand of thread.
- No 9 straw or millinery needles for one strand of thread.

AGAPANTHUS *Agapanthus orientalis*

THREADS

340   blue violet – medium
341   blue violet – light
3346 hunter green

STRANDS AND STITCHES USED

flowers	1 strand each 340 and 341 blended, fly stitch
stems	2 strands 3346, whipped stem stitch
leaves	2 strands 3346, stem stitch

Lightly mark arched leaves and stems. Draw a circle at the top of each stem, leaving a small segment where the flower joins the stem. The flowers are worked in fly stitch with a small 'V' on the outside of the circle and the long tail going into the same hole in the centre. Work in a clockwise direction and stagger the length of the stitches. A few straight stitches in one strand of 3346 radiating from the centre will give a realistic effect. The stems are worked in a single row of whipped stem stitch and the arched leaves in two rows of stem stitch tapering to a point. Cross some leaves over the stems and other leaves. A bud can be added in satin stitch, if desired.

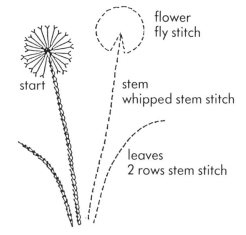

start

flower
fly stitch

stem
whipped stem stitch

leaves
2 rows stem stitch

ALYSSUM (SWEET ALICE) *Lobularia maritima*

THREADS

blanc neige
3051   green grey – dark

STRANDS AND STITCHES USED

flowers   1 strand blanc neige, French knots
leaves   1 strand 3051, straight stitch

Flowers are worked in clusters of six to eight French knots with a few small straight stitches around the edge. Alysum is useful for filling in spaces between other flowers.

leaves
straight stitch

flowers
French knots

COTTAGE PINKS *Dianthus plumarius*

THREADS

blanc neige
819   baby pink – light
503   blue green – medium

STRANDS AND STITCHES USED

stems	2 strands 503, stem stitch
leaves	2 strands 503, straight stitch
flowers	1 strand each blanc neige and 819 blended, straight stitch
buds	1 strand 819, bullion stitch

Lightly mark stems and work in stem stitch. Work leaves in straight stitch at base of plant and on the stems. Flowers are worked in straight stitch (not too many), working from the outside into the same hole in the centre. Vary the length of the stitches to give a realistic look. Buds are worked in bullion stitch of nine wraps and are scattered throughout the foliage.

flowers
straight stitch

buds
bullion stitch

stems
stem stitch

leaves
straight stitch

CYCLAMEN *Cyclamen sp.*

Note: There are two colours for this flower.

THREADS

blanc neige
or
335   rose

501   blue green – dark
503   blue green – medium

STRANDS AND STITCHES USED

leaves   1 strand each 501 and 503 blended, buttonhole stitch
flowers   2 strands blanc neige or 335, lazy daisy stitch
stems   1 strand 501, stem stitch

First work clusters of heart-shaped leaves in buttonhole stitch. Work flowers above the leaves using two or three lazy daisy stitches overlapping slightly from the same point and pointing upwards or fanning to the side. Work stems in stem stitch offset slightly from the centre of the flower. Check illustration for position.

flowers
lazy daisy stitch

stems
stem stitch

leaves
buttonhole stitch

DAFFODIL *Narcissus sp.*

THREADS

743   yellow – medium
745   yellow – light pale
372   mustard – light
3363 pine green – medium

STRANDS AND STITCHES USED

stems and leaves	2 strands 3363, stem stitch
flowers trumpet	2 strands 743, buttonhole stitch
petals	2 strands 745, lazy daisy stitch
bracts	2 strands 372, lazy daisy stitch

Lightly mark stems and leaves and work in stem stitch. The aura of realism can be enhanced by working some leaves so that they bend at an angle. Work the trumpet of the daffodil using three buttonhole stitches commencing from the left-hand side of the outside edge. Place two or three lazy daisy stitch petals at the top of the trumpet. Work one lazy daisy stitch for the bract to attach flower to stem.

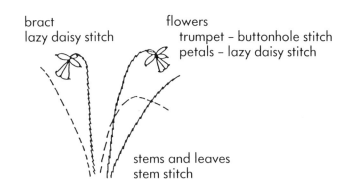

bract
lazy daisy stitch

flowers
trumpet – buttonhole stitch
petals – lazy daisy stitch

stems and leaves
stem stitch

start

DAPHNE *Daphne odora*

THREADS

blanc neige
316   antique mauve – medium
611   drab brown – dark
987   forest green – dark

STRANDS AND STITCHES USED

flowers   1 strand each blanc neige and 316 blended, French knots
leaves   2 strands 987, lazy daisy stitch
branches   2 strands 611, long bullion stitch

Mark placement of flowers. Some flowers are worked before placement of branches and others after placement, so a few of the leaves can overlap the branches to create a more realistic-looking shrub. Work flowers in clusters of seven to 10 French knots surrounded by approximately seven to 10 lazy daisy leaves. The number of wraps for the bullion stitch branches will vary depending on the length required. Work on the basis that an average of 10 wraps measures approximately 6 mm (¼″), and 50 wraps approximately 33 mm (1¼″). The long bullion stitch branches are couched into position.

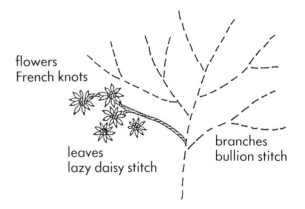

flowers
French knots

leaves
lazy daisy stitch

branches
bullion stitch

DELPHINIUM *Delphinium elatum*

Each flower is worked in a different shade of blue. To give a sense of perspective, place the palest shade of flower in the background and the darkest shade in the foreground.

THREADS

792   cornflower blue – dark
793   cornflower blue – medium
794   cornflower blue – light
987   forest green – dark

STRANDS AND STITCHES USED

buds	3 strands 987, French knots
	2 strands blue and 1 strand 987 blended, French knots
flowers	3 strands and 4 strands 792, French knots, or
	3 strands and 4 strands 793, French knots, or
	3 strands and 4 strands 794, French knots
leaves	2 strands 987, lazy daisy stitch

The use of a small embroidery hoop when working these flowers will make your task far quicker and easier. Mark three conical shapes for your tall delphiniums. Work buds closely in French knots from the top, working down with three strands of green, then two strands of the chosen blue blended with one strand of green. Graduate to three strands of blue. Do not finish in a straight line but blend each new thread combination. Continue down the flower changing to four strands of blue towards the base. Place lazy daisy leaves around the base of the flowers, if necessary or desired. As these flowers grow very tall and are time-consuming to work, they are ideal for placing behind other flowers.

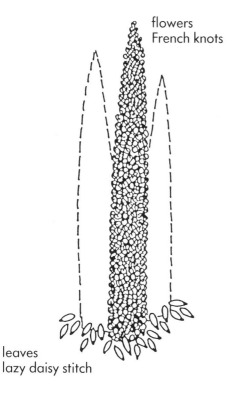

flowers
French knots

leaves
lazy daisy stitch

DUTCH HYACINTH *Hyacinthus orientalis*

THREADS

963   dusty rose – very light
3689   mauve – light
3347   yellow green – medium

STRANDS AND STITCHES USED

| stem and leaves | 3 strands 3347, straight stitch |
| flowers | 2 strands 963 and 1 strand 3689 blended, French knots |

Sew one long straight stitch as stem with two shorter straight stitches either side as leaves. Work French knots closely down either side and over the stem to form a rectangular shape.

flowers
French knots

stems and leaves
straight stitch

ENGLISH BLUEBELL
Endymion nonscriptus (previously *Scilla nonscripta*)

THREADS

341   blue violet – light
3346 hunter green

STRANDS AND STITCHES USED

flowers	2 strands 341, buttonhole stitch
stems	2 strands 3346, couching
leaves	2 strands 3346, stem stitch

Lightly draw in stems; leave a generous space between stems (the flowers take up more space than you might at first think). Stems are worked in couching. Work flowers from the bottom in alternate bells of two buttonhole stitches on either side of the stem. Just one bell is worked on the top of the flower to form a point. Add leaves in stem stitch.

stems
couching

flowers
buttonhole stitch

leaves
stem stitch

ENGLISH PRIMROSE *Primula vulgaris*

THREADS

745   yellow – light pale
612   drab brown – medium
471   avocado green – very light

STRANDS AND STITCHES USED

flowers	petals	2 strands 745, lazy daisy stitch
	centre	2 strands 612, French knot
stems		2 strands 471, stem stitch or couching
leaves		2 strands 471, lazy daisy stitch

Work flowers with five petals in lazy daisy stitch radiating from the centre. Some flowers may only have four petals, depicting a side view. Place a French knot in the centre of each flower. Work stems in stem stitch or couching and sew lazy daisy leaves randomly around the base.

flowers
lazy daisy stitch

stems
couching

centre
French knot

leaves
lazy daisy stitch

FLOWERING ALMOND CHERRY (PRUNUS)
Prunus glandulosa 'Rosa'

THREADS

3689	mauve – light
605	cranberry – very light
610	drab brown – very dark
988	forest green – medium

STRANDS AND STITCHES USED

branches	2 strands 610, couching
minor branches	1 strand 610, straight stitch
flowers	2 strands 605 and 1 strand 3689 blended, French knots
leaves	1 strand 988, straight stitch

Lightly draw in branches and couch. Add minor branches in straight stitch. Cover heavily with French knot flowers and place leaves throughout in small straight stitches.

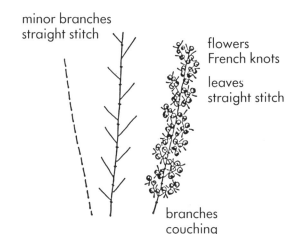

minor branches
straight stitch

flowers
French knots

leaves
straight stitch

branches
couching

FORGET-ME-NOT *Myosotis sylvatica*

There is a choice of three colours for these flowers.

THREADS

800	delft – pale
or	
3354	dusty rose – light
or	
809	delft
726	topaz – light
989	forest green

STRANDS AND STITCHES USED

flowers	centre	2 strands 726, French knots
	petals	2 strands 800 or 3354 or 809, French knots
leaves		2 strands 989, lazy daisy stitch

Work centres first in one French knot and surround very closely with five French knots for petals. Scatter lazy daisy stitch leaves sparingly underneath the flowers.

flowers
French knots

leaves
lazy daisy stitch

FORSYTHIA *Forsythia suspensa*

THREADS

726   topaz – light
372   mustard – light
730   olive green – very dark

STRANDS AND STITCHES USED

branches   2 strands 372, stem stitch
leaves   2 strands 730, lazy daisy stitch
flowers   2 strands 726, small straight stitch

Lightly draw in branches and work in stem stitch. Work two or three leaves in lazy daisy stitch from the top of the branches, pointing upwards. Flowers are worked in two or three small straight stitches either side of, and over, the branches, approximately every 5 mm ($\frac{1}{5}$") and angled out and downwards.

   Forsythia designed by Tineke Mitter.

leaves
lazy daisy stitch

branches
stem stitch

flowers
straight stitch

FOXGLOVE *Digitalis purpurea*

THREADS

225   shell pink – very light
224   shell pink – light
223   shell pink – medium
3363 pine green – medium

STRANDS AND STITCHES USED

stems	2 strands 3363, stem stitch or couching
buds	2 strands 3363, French knots
	1 strand 3363 and 225 blended, French knots 2 twists
flowers	2 strands 225, 2 buttonhole stitches
	1 strand 225 and 224 blended, 3 buttonhole stitches
	2 strands 224, 3 buttonhole stitches
	1 strand 224 and 223 blended, 3 buttonhole stitches
	2 strands 223, 3 buttonhole stitches (if required or desired)
leaves	2 strands 3363, satin stitch

Mark stems and work in couching or stem stitch, starting at the base. With the same thread, at the top of the stem work three or four buds in French knots. Finish off. Do not extend thread across to the next stem: the green thread will show through your work. Stitch four or five buds in the blended threads in French knots (two twists).

The flowers are worked from the top of the stem, graduating in colour as listed above. Work five or six trumpets in each thread combination. Before commencing, please check where to start on flower illustration. Work trumpets from left to right, placing on either side of the stem, crossing over stems and staggering them as you work down. Add an extra trumpet to the side and centre here and there. They should be slightly longer and placed more thickly at the base of the stem.

Draw elongated leaves with a central vein. Stitch outline in one strand of green in small running stitch. Work leaf in satin stitch: use very slanting stitches and, starting at leaf base, work along one side of leaf, straightening stitches to form a point. Then work back down the other side. For those who don't like satin stitch, these leaves can be worked in an elongated satin leaf stitch.

Foxgloves can also be worked behind other flowers; the inclusion of leaves is then unnecessary.

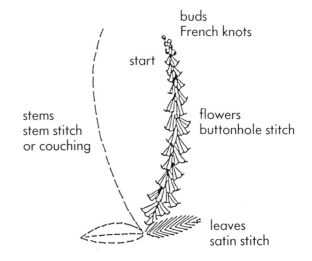

buds
French knots

start

stems
stem stitch
or couching

flowers
buttonhole stitch

leaves
satin stitch

FRENCH LAVENDER *Lavandula dentata*

THREADS

208   lavender – very dark
3053 green grey

STRANDS AND STITCHES USED

foliage	2 strands 3053, fly stitch
flower heads	1 strand each 208 and 3053 blended, bullion stitch

Lightly mark foliage. Work each branch starting at the top with a straight stitch and work down in fly stitch to the base. Overlap some branches and stitch some smaller branches for a realistic-looking lavender bush.

Work flower heads, following the angle of the stem, in bullion stitch (nine wraps) at the top of each branch. Scatter more throughout the foliage. To stitch a pointed lavender head, take the needle out a little further when anchoring the bullion stitch.

flower heads
bullion stitch

foliage
fly stitch

GRAPE HYACINTH *Muscari armeniacum*

THREADS

333   blue violet – dark
3052   green grey – medium

STRANDS AND STITCHES USED

stems   2 strands 3052, couching
flowers   2 strands 333, French knots

Lightly mark stems and couch. Work French knots down either side and over the stem starting at the peak and increasing to the base, forming an elongated conical shape. Do not work these flowers too closely together as they tend to lose their shape and become just a blur of blue.

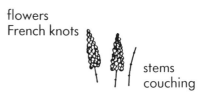

flowers
French knots

stems
couching

GYPSOPHILA (BABY'S BREATH) *Gypsophila elegans*

THREADS

blanc neige
3347   yellow green – medium

STRANDS AND STITCHES USED

foliage   1 strand 3347, fly stitch
flowers   2 strands blanc neige, French knots

Lightly mark an area for the foliage and work in fly stitch. Flowers are worked in clusters of French knots at the top of the foliage, with more scattered throughout.

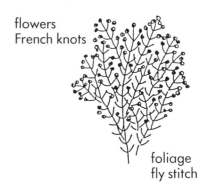

flowers
French knots

foliage
fly stitch

HEART'S-EASE (JOHNNY JUMP-UP) *Viola tricolor*

THREADS

444   lemon – dark
211   lavender – light
727   topaz – very light
333   blue violet – dark
469   avocado green

STRANDS AND STITCHES USED

flowers	lower petal	2 strands 444, buttonhole stitch
	side petals	1 strand each 727 and 211 blended, lazy daisy stitch
	top petals	2 strands 333, lazy daisy stitch
leaves		2 strands 469, lazy daisy stitch

These flowers are very tiny, so the stitches need to be kept as small as possible. Begin with the lower petal using three buttonhole stitches. Work side petals pointing to the sides and top petals pointing upwards in lazy daisy stitch coming from the centre. Leaves in lazy daisy stitch are scattered randomly around the flowers.

leaves
lazy daisy stitch

flowers
buttonhole stitch
and lazy daisy stitch

start

HOLLYHOCK *Alcea rosea* (previously *Althaea rosea*)

THREADS

335   rose
962   dusty rose – medium
3364 pine green

STRANDS AND STITCHES USED

flowers	outer petals	2 strands 962, buttonhole stitch
	centres	3 strands 335, French knots
	buds	2 strands 3364, French knots, 2 twists
		2 strands 335, French knots, 2 twists
opening flower		2 strands 335, 5 buttonhole stitches
calyx		2 strands 3364, fly stitch
stem		2 strands 3364, stem stitch
leaves		2 strands 3364, satin leaf stitch

Lightly mark stem and then placement of flowers – an inner and outer circle graduating in size from large at the base to smaller at the top. These flowers are not completely circular but slightly irregular in shape. Work outer circle in buttonhole stitch and inner circle in French knots.

Work stem in stem stitch from the base upwards, connecting each flower head. Two rows can be worked for the lower stem. Extend the stem; hollyhocks are very tall plants and can grow to 2.5 metres (8′).

Sew the buds with French knots (two twists) alternating the colours of green and pink around the top of the stem.

The uppermost opening flowers are worked with a segment of buttonhole stitch (five stitches) attached to the stem with a calyx in fly stitch. It is easier to turn your work upside down to sew these half-opened flowers.

Leaves are worked in satin leaf stitch at the base of your hollyhock, with smaller ones between the flowers.

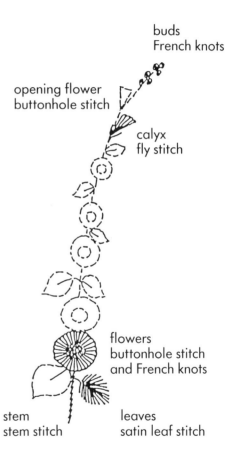

buds
French knots

opening flower
buttonhole stitch

calyx
fly stitch

flowers
buttonhole stitch
and French knots

stem
stem stitch

leaves
satin leaf stitch

LILY-OF-THE-VALLEY *Convallaria majalis*

THREADS

blanc neige
3347   yellow green – medium

STRANDS AND STITCHES USED

flowers	2 strands blanc neige, French knots
stems	1 strand 3347, stem stitch
leaves	2 strands 3347, satin stitch outlined in 1 strand stem stitch

Lightly mark arched stem and two leaves. Leaves are worked in a very slanting satin stitch and are outlined with one strand of stem stitch. Work stems in stem stitch and add French knot flowers over the stem.

stems
stem stitch

flowers
French knots

leaves
satin stitch
outline – stem stitch

MAGNOLIA *Magnolia x soulangeana*

THREADS

blanc neige
316   antique mauve – medium
839   beige brown – dark
840   beige brown – medium
3013 khaki green – light

STRANDS AND STITCHES USED

tree	2 strands 839, stem stitch
	2 strands 840, stem stitch
flowers	2 strands blanc neige and 1 strand 316 blended double lazy daisy stitch
calyxes	2 strands 3013, fly stitch
leaf buds	2 strands 3013, bullion stitch

Draw in the trunk and branches of the tree and work in stem stitch in 839. Sew a second row in 840 stem stitch for the trunk and major branches. A third row in 840 may be added for the trunk if desired.

Flowers are worked in large, loose, double lazy daisy stitch with the stitches overlapping. Some should have three petals, and some four for variation. A straight stitch can be added if there is a gap in the centre of the double lazy daisy stitch. Work a few flower buds with one large double lazy daisy stitch.

Attach flowers to branches with a calyx in fly stitch. Scatter leaf buds over the tree, worked in bullion stitch (nine wraps), anchoring the thread further out to form an elongated point.

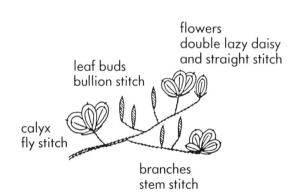

flowers
double lazy daisy
and straight stitch

leaf buds
bullion stitch

calyx
fly stitch

branches
stem stitch

PERIWINKLE *Vinca major*

THREADS

209   lavender – dark
3346 hunter green

STRANDS AND STITCHES USED

stems	2 strands 3346, couching
leaves	2 strands 3346, lazy daisy stitch
flowers	2 strands 209, lazy daisy stitch
buds	1 strand 209, bullion stitch

Lightly mark stems and stitch in couching. Work lazy daisy stitch leaves in pairs along stems. Work flowers of five petals in small lazy daisy stitch at the top of the stem and scatter a few through the foliage. Place the occasional bud using bullion stitch (nine wraps). Extend the needle out slightly when anchoring the bullion, to give an elongated and curved effect.

buds
bullion stitch

flowers
lazy daisy stitch

stems
couching

leaves
lazy daisy stitch

ROSE (STANDARD) *Rosa*

THREADS

221   shell pink – dark
223   shell pink – medium
3051 green grey – dark
937   avocado green – medium

STRANDS AND STITCHES USED

trunk		2 strands 3051, stem stitch
flowers	centres	2 strands 221, bullion stitch
	outside petals	2 strands 223, bullion stitch
leaves		2 strands 3051, lazy daisy stitch
		2 strands 937, lazy daisy stitch

Draw in the trunk approximately 3-4 cm (1¼″-1½″) long and mark a circle at the top (a cotton reel is a good size). Work the trunk in two rows of stem stitch.

Mark the placement of roses scattered over the circle – 13 roses are sufficient. Work the centre of roses in two bullion stitches (nine wraps) starting and finishing at the same point at either end. Work bullion stitch outer petals (11 wraps) curving around the centre on either side.

Work lazy daisy leaves in the two shades of green in a sunburst radiating from the centre of the circle to the outside edge. Vary the length and direction of the leaves.

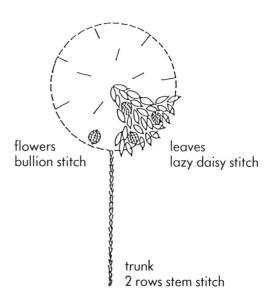

flowers
bullion stitch

leaves
lazy daisy stitch

trunk
2 rows stem stitch

SHASTA DAISY *Chrysanthemum superbum*

THREADS

blanc neige
444   lemon – dark
3347 yellow green – medium

STRANDS AND STITCHES USED

flowers	centres	2 strands 444, French knots
	petals	2 strands blanc neige, lazy daisy stitch
stems		2 strands 3347, couching
stem leaves		2 strands 3347, straight stitch
leaves		2 strands 3347, lazy daisy stitch

Lightly mark flowers with a small circle surrounded by a larger circle. Work centre with five French knots. Divide outer circle into quarters like a clock face. Work one lazy daisy stitch petal for the 12 o'clock position and each quarter, and then fill in between these with more petals. This will prevent a pinwheel effect. The more petals you have the better it will look. Mark in stems and couch. Work small straight stitch leaves angled downwards and alternating at intervals on each side down the stem. Work leaves of lazy daisy stitches at random around the base. A half flower adds interest.

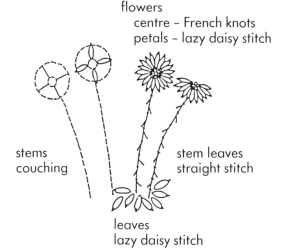

flowers
centre – French knots
petals – lazy daisy stitch

stems
couching

stem leaves
straight stitch

leaves
lazy daisy stitch

SNOWFLAKE *Leucojum vernum*

THREADS

blanc neige
3347 yellow green – medium

STRANDS AND STITCHES USED

stems and leaves	2 strands 3347, stem stitch
flowers	2 strands blanc neige, lazy daisy stitch
flower spots	1 strand 3347, French knots

Draw in stems and leaves and work in stem stitch. Work very small flowers in 'bunches' of two or three lazy daisy stitches down one side of the stem or over the stem. Place a French knot for the flower spot in each of the lazy daisy petals.

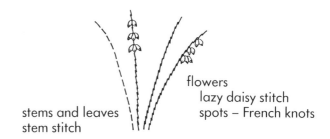

stems and leaves
stem stitch

flowers
lazy daisy stitch
spots – French knots

SOLOMON'S SEAL *Polygonatum multiflorum*

THREADS

blanc neige
3348   yellow green – light
3347   yellow green — medium

STRANDS AND STITCHES USED

stems	2 strands 3347, stem stitch
leaves	2 strands 3347, lazy daisy stitch
flower stalks	1 strand 3347, straight stitch
flowers	1 strand blanc neige, lazy daisy stitch
flower tip	1 strand 3348, French knots

Mark arched stem and work in stem stitch. Work lazy daisy leaves along the top edge of the stem; there should be approximately 16 leaves. Place very small flower stalks pointing downwards from each of the leaves underneath the arching stem. Work two or three flowers from each flower stalk in lazy daisy stitch pointing downwards. The green flower tip is worked with a French knot: bring the needle up inside the lower end of each lazy daisy flower, finishing below the flower.

leaves
lazy daisy stitch

flowers
lazy daisy stitch
tips – French knots
stalks – straight stitch

stem
stem stitch

VIOLET (SWEET) *Viola odorata*

Note: Two colours are given for this flower.

THREADS

327   antique violet – dark
or
333   blue violet – dark

3346 hunter green *or* 987 forest green – dark
743   yellow – medium

STRANDS AND STITCHES USED

leaves	1 strand 3346, buttonhole stitch
flowers	1 strand 327, lazy daisy stitch
bud	1 strand 327, lazy daisy stitch
centres	2 strands 743, French knots
calyx	1 strand 3346, fly stitch
stems	1 strand 3346, stem stitch

First work clusters of heart-shaped leaves in buttonhole stitch. Flowers consist of three lazy daisy stitch petals fanning from the centre and pointing downwards, and two lazy daisy stitch petals pointing upwards. Place a French knot in the centre. Buds have only two lazy daisy stitches pointing downwards with a calyx of fly stitch. Work stems in stem stitch, arching them at the top where the flower is attached.

flowers
lazy daisy stitch
centre – French knot

stems
stem stitch

buds
lazy daisy stitch

leaves
buttonhole stitch

WINTER ROSE (HELLEBORUS)
Helleborus orientalis

THREADS

316   antique mauve – medium
3052   green grey – medium
3346   hunter green

STRANDS AND STITCHES USED

flowers   2 strands 316, lazy daisy stitch
           1 strand each 316 and 3052 blended, lazy daisy stitch
leaves   1 strand each 3052 and 3346 blended, lazy daisy stitch

Lightly mark dome-shaped area. The pink and pink/green flowers are worked first and scattered over the area. Work flowers in three lazy daisy stitches from the same hole, fanning downwards. Work leaves in two small lazy daisy stitches pointing upward from the centre top of the flower. Cluster lazy daisy leaves densely around the base and scatter a few leaves through the flowers, if necessary.

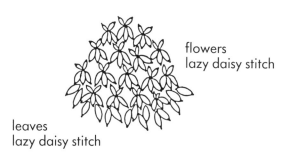

flowers
lazy daisy stitch

leaves
lazy daisy stitch

WISTERIA *Wisteria sinensis*

THREADS

208   lavender – very dark
210   lavender – medium
640   beige grey – very dark
3013 khaki green – light
3348 yellow green – medium

STRANDS AND STITCHES USED

vine	2 strands 640, stem stitch
flower stalks	2 strands 3348, coral stitch
flowers	2 strands 208, French knots
	1 strand each 208 and 210 blended, French knots
	3 strands 210, French knots
leaf stalks	2 strands 3348, coral stitch
leaves	1 strand each 3013 and 3348 blended, lazy daisy stitch

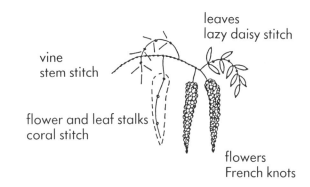

leaves
lazy daisy stitch

vine
stem stitch

flower and leaf stalks
coral stitch

flowers
French knots

Mark vine on pergola and work in stem stitch. The thicker part of the vine is worked with two rows of stem stitch.

Mark placement of flower stalks and work in coral stitch. Some of the coral stitch will be covered by flowers but the top 5 mm (¹⁄₅″) will form the stalk. The coral stitch knots will peep through the flowers.

Commence working the flowers at the tip and work upwards in French knots using the different thread combinations as listed above, starting with 208. The bulk of the flowers will be worked in the three strands of 210. Make sure the flowers do not become too wide; they should be long and pendulous; they should not resemble bunches of grapes. Some people prefer to work these flowers from the top down to the tip.

The leaf stalks curve from the vine and are worked in coral stitch. The leaves are worked in pairs of lazy daisy stitches (nine to 11 leaves).

PUSSY CAT

THREADS

452   shell grey – medium

STRANDS AND STITCHES USED

body	2 strands, long and short stitch
head	2 strands, satin stitch
tail	2 strands, stem stitch
ears	2 strands, satin stitch
outline	1 strand, stem stitch

Draw a simple outline of a cat. Work body in long and short stitch, head and ears in satin stitch and long tail tapering to a point in two rows stem stitch. Outline body and head in 1 strand stem stitch.

head
satin stitch

body
long and short stitch

outline
stem stitch

tail
stem stitch

BUTTERFLY

THREADS

341   blue violet – light
452   shell grey – medium

STRANDS AND STITCHES USED

wings	2 strands 341, long and short stitch
body	2 strands 452, bullion stitch
feelers	1 strand 452, stem stitch
outline	1 strand 452, stem stitch

Draw outline of butterfly and work wings in long and short stitch. Work body between the wings in bullion stitch (13 wraps). Couch in position to form head and body. Outline wings in one strand 452 stem stitch and place feelers at top of head arching outwards.

feelers and outline
stem stitch

wings
long and short stitch

body
bullion stitch

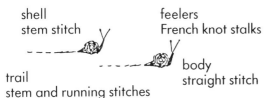

shell
stem stitch

feelers
French knot stalks

body
straight stitch

trail
stem and running stitches

SNAIL

THREADS

612   drab brown – medium
420   hazelnut brown – dark
762   pearl grey – very light

STRANDS AND STITCHES USED

shell	1 strand each 612 and 420 blended, stem stitch
head and tail	1 strand 420, straight stitch
feelers	1 strand 420, French knot stalk
trail	1 strand 762, stem and running stitch

Work shell in stem stitch starting in the centre and work around in an anti-clockwise direction until a small spiral of desired size is achieved. Work head and tail in straight stitch and feelers on top of head in French knot stalk. Work trail leading away from snail in stem stitch with a few running stitches tapering off into the foliage. Remember that the snail is very small.

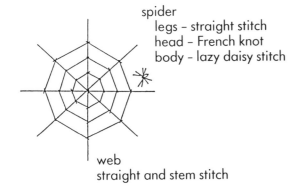

spider
legs – straight stitch
head – French knot
body – lazy daisy stitch

web
straight and stem stitch

SPIDER AND WEB

THREADS

762   pearl grey – light
611   drab brown – dark

STRANDS AND STITCHES USED

web		1 strand 762, straight and stem stitch
spider	head	1 strand 611, French knots, 2 twists
	body	1 strand 611, lazy daisy stitch
	legs	1 strand 611, straight stitch

Find a suitable position for the web where the spokes can attach to the foliage or flowers. Work eight spokes in long straight stitches crossing over in the centre; couch at this point. Work a long stem stitch over each of the spokes in a circular manner. The number of times this is done depends on the size of the web – do at least three.

The spider is very tiny. Work the head first in one French knot (two twists) and the body in a lazy daisy stitch. Place eight legs in straight stitch, four on either side of the head.

FLAGSTONES

THREADS

612   drab brown – medium

STRANDS AND STITCHES USED

1 strand, stem stitch

Mark flagstones and work in 1 strand stem stitch.

PERGOLA

THREADS

611   drab brown – dark

STRANDS AND STITCHES USED

2 strands, stem stitch

Draw in outline of pergola and work in stem stitch. Flowers and leaves will cover some parts of the pergola.

Reference – Macoboy, S. *Stirling Macoboy's What Flower is That?* Weldon Publishing, 1989.

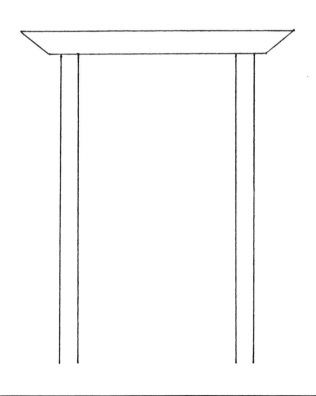

CHAPTER 12

STITCH GLOSSARY

Embroidery stitches have many different names and feature variations in structure and technique of working. This glossary describes how the stitches have been worked for the designs in this book.

For left-handed embroiderers, the instructions should be reversed. To make this easier, a mirror-image of the diagrams may prove helpful.

STEM OR OUTLINE STITCH

A simple stitch for stems, outlines and filling.

Working from left to right, take small, even straight or slightly slanting stitches along the design line. Leave a space between the point where the needle emerges and the previous stitch. Keep the thread below or on the same side of your work. For wide stem stitch, make the stitches on a greater angle.

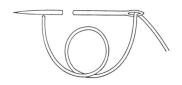

Stem or outline stitch

WHIPPED STEM STITCH

Whipped stem stitch gives a corded effect.

Work a row of stem stitch along the design line and bring the needle to the top of your work. Work in the opposite direction to that of the stem stitch. With the blunt end of the needle whip back through each stem stitch, but not into the fabric.

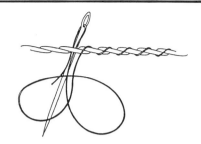

Whipped stem stitch

COUCHING

The branches and flower stems in this book worked in couching have two strands of thread laid down and one strand for the tying stitch of matching thread. Use two needles and keep them on top of your work to prevent tangling. Anchor the thread not in use and keep it out of the way.

Lay the thread along the design line, holding and guiding its direction with your thumb. Tie it down with small straight stitches made at regular intervals.

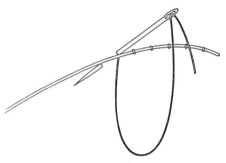

Couching

CORAL STITCH

Coral stitch is a simple knotted line stitch useful for flower stems.

Hold the thread to the left along the design line. Take a small stitch towards you with the thread over and around the needle; pull through forming a knot. Continue at regular intervals.

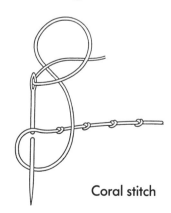

Coral stitch

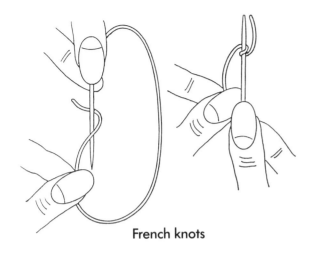

French knots

FRENCH KNOTS

When working French knots you will have more control and be able to develop a rhythm if a small (10 cm/4″) hoop is used. To increase the size of knots, use more strands of thread.

Bring the thread up at the desired spot. Hold the thread firmly with your left hand. With the needle pointing toward you, place it under the thread from the left-hand side and twist it around once. Insert the needle close to where the thread first emerged, but not in the same hole. Draw the thread around the needle to firm the knot and pull through to the back. Pass on to the position for the next knot.

FRENCH KNOT STALKS

French knot stalks are worked in the same manner as French knots.

To form the stalk, after encircling the needle with the thread, insert the needle the desired distance away from where it first emerged. Pull through to the back, taking care with tension.

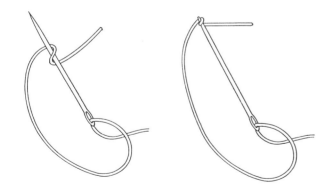

French knot stalks

BULLION STITCH

This stitch should be worked with a straw or millinery needle. The small eye will allow the needle to pass easily through the wraps. The number of wraps should equal the length of the back stitch.

Make a back stitch the required length for the bullion stitch. Bring the needle up at the starting point but do not pull through. Wrap the thread around the needle, in a clockwise direction, the required number of times. Do not wrap too tightly. Place your left thumb over the wraps, then pull the needle through the wraps. As you pull the thread up firmly, the bullion will turn back. Adjust the wraps if necessary. Insert the needle at the starting point and pull through to complete the bullion stitch.

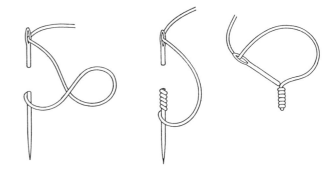

Bullion stitch

LAZY DAISY OR DETACHED CHAIN

This is a very useful stitch for leaves and flower petals.

Bring the needle through at the point where you wish to begin your stitch. Hold the thread below your work and insert the needle close to where the thread first emerged. Bring the needle out at the desired distance, keeping the thread underneath. Fasten the loop at the end with a small straight stitch. Pass on to the beginning of the next stitch.

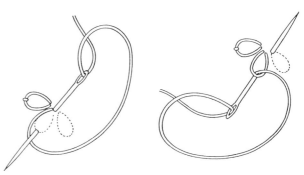

Lazy daisy or detached chain

DOUBLE LAZY DAISY STITCH

This stitch is useful for leaves and large flower petals. It can be worked in two colours.

The inside stitch is worked first as an ordinary lazy daisy stitch. The larger second stitch is worked outside and around the first stitch.

Double lazy daisy stitch

FLY STITCH

Fly stitch is an open lazy daisy stitch. The tying stitch can vary in length as required. It can be worked singly, vertically, horizontally or radiating into a circle.

Bring the thread through at the top left of your design. Insert the needle a little distance away to the right and take a small diagonal stitch to the centre with the thread below the needle. Pull through and fasten with a straight downward stitch.

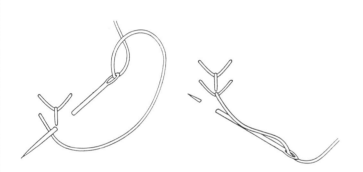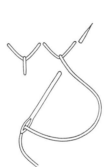

Fly stitch

BUTTONHOLE STITCH

This stitch is the same as blanket stitch but the stitches are worked closer together. It can be worked in a row or a circle.

Start on the outside edge and work from left to right. Hold the thread below and take a downward straight stitch and draw up with the thread underneath the needle. Continue in this way, spacing stitches as required.

SATIN STITCH - SLANTED

This stitch should be worked with even stitches to cover the fabric completely, resulting in a smooth finish. Work with a stabbing motion for better tension. The use of a hoop will help.

A running stitch may be worked first to outline the design. This will help to form a good edge. Work slanting stitches closely together across the area outlined.

STRAIGHT STITCH

Straight stitch is a single satin stitch and can be worked in any direction and to any length. Take care with the tension. Do not make the stitches too long otherwise snagging may occur.

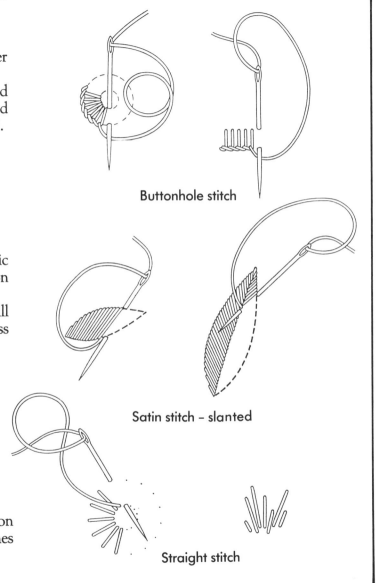

Buttonhole stitch

Satin stitch - slanted

Straight stitch

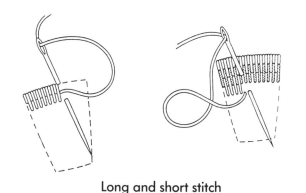

Long and short stitch

LONG AND SHORT SATIN STITCH

This stitch can be used to fill areas too large to be covered by satin stitch. It can also be used to achieve subtle shading.

Work the first row in alternate long and short satin stitches. Closely follow the outline of the design shape. The following rows are then worked in long stitches in a brick fashion until the area is filled.

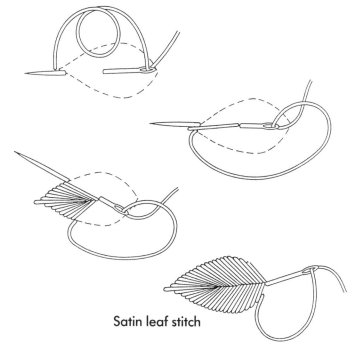

Satin leaf stitch

SATIN LEAF STITCH

This variation of satin stitch is easy to work and forms a very realistic leaf. It is taken from Brazilian embroidery.

The first stitch should be a little longer than you might expect, in order to form a good point on the leaf. Work the first satin stitch from the point of the leaf back into the centre of the leaf. Bring the needle back up on the left of the first stitch at the leaf tip. Take this second stitch back to the central leaf vein and insert the needle just below, but very close to the first stitch. Work the satin stitches alternately from each side fanning them as the leaf forms. At the same time, continue to work closely down the central vein. You may need to add one or two extra stitches on one side of your leaf if it is not symmetrical.

STARTING AND FINISHING

The use of a small knot is quite an acceptable and secure way to begin your work.

There are many satisfactory ways to finish off your thread. The following method is used for smocking and is neat and secure.

Take a small stitch to form a loop. Pass the needle through the loop to form a second loop. Pass the needle through the second loop and pull up tightly to form a secure knot.

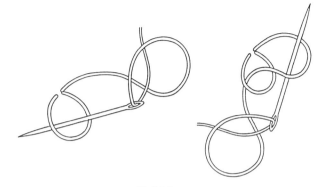

Finishing

NOTES ON THE
APPENDICES

Prerequisites for Cottage Garden,
Spring Garden and Spring Garland

DMC STRANDED COTTON

A complete list of flowers and colour numbers has been given for each of the three designs. Some colours overlap from one flower to another. However, one skein of stranded cotton is sufficient to complete a design.

Many flowers are common to all three designs. Should you intend to do all these designs, check these flowers and the colour numbers as you will not need to duplicate all the threads for each individual design.

No list has been provided for the embroidered initials as the choice of flowers is a personal one and all colour numbers are listed in the Flower Glossary.

COTTAGE GARDEN

agapanthus	French lavender
alyssum	gypsophila
cottage pinks	heart's-ease
cyclamen	hollyhock
delphinium	periwinkle
English primrose	rose
forget-me-not	shasta daisy
foxglove	violet

SPRING GARDEN

cyclamen	grape hyacinth
daffodil	lily-of-the-valley
Daphne	magnolia
Dutch hyacinth	periwinkle
English bluebell	snowflake
English primrose	Solomon's seal
flowering almond cherry	violet
forget-me-not	Winter rose
French lavender	wisteria

SPRING GARLAND

cyclamen	lily-of-the-valley
Daphne	magnolia
English primrose	periwinkle
forget-me-not	violet
forsythia	Winter rose
French lavender	wisteria

APPENDIX A
COTTAGE GARDEN

THREADS

blanc neige
208	lavender – very dark
209	lavender – dark
211	lavender – light
221	shell pink – dark
223	shell pink – medium
224	shell pink – light
225	shell pink – very light
327	antique violet – dark
333	blue violet – dark
335	rose
340	blue violet – medium
341	blue violet – light
444	lemon – dark
469	avocado green – light
471	avocado green – very light
501	blue green – dark
503	blue green – medium
611	drab brown – dark
612	drab brown – medium
726	topaz – light
727	topaz – very light
743	yellow – medium
745	yellow – light pale
762	pearl grey – very light
792	cornflower blue – dark

793	cornflower blue – medium
794	cornflower blue – light
800	delft – pale
809	delft
819	baby pink – light
937	avocado green – medium
962	dusty rose – medium
987	forest green – dark
989	forest green
3051	green grey – dark
3053	green grey
3346	hunter green
3347	yellow green – medium
3354	dusty rose – light
3363	pine green – medium
3364	pine green

NEEDLES

Embroidery crewel Nos 7, 8 and 9
Straw or millinery Nos 8 and 9

FABRIC

45 cm x 27 cm (18" x 11")

Small embroidery hoop 10 cm (4")
Soft pencil and small embroidery
scissors

APPENDIX B
SPRING GARDEN

THREADS

blanc neige		963	dusty rose – very light
208	lavender – very dark	987	forest green – dark
209	lavender – dark	988	forest green – medium
210	lavender – medium	989	forest green
316	antique mauve – medium	3013	khaki green – light
327	antique violet – dark	3052	green grey – medium
333	blue violet – dark	3053	green grey
341	blue violet – light	3346	hunter green
372	mustard – light	3347	yellow green – medium
420	hazelnut brown – dark	3348	yellow green – light
452	shell grey – medium	3363	pine green – medium
471	avocado green – very light	3689	mauve – light
501	blue green – dark		
503	blue green – medium		
605	cranberry – very light	NEEDLES	
610	drab brown – very dark		
611	drab brown – dark	Embroidery crewel Nos 7, 8 and 9	
612	drab brown – medium	Straw or millinery Nos 8 and 9	
640	beige grey – very dark		
726	topaz – light		
743	yellow – medium	FABRIC	
745	yellow – light pale		
762	pearl grey – very light	45 cm x 27 cm (18″ x 11″)	
800	delft – pale		
839	beige brown – dark	Small embroidery hoop 10 cm (4″)	
840	beige brown – medium	Soft pencil and small embroidery scissors	

APPENDIX C
SPRING GARLAND

THREADS

blanc neige	
208	lavender – very dark
209	lavender – dark
210	lavender – medium
316	antique mauve – medium
327	antique violet – dark
341	blue violet – light
372	mustard – light
452	shell grey – medium
471	avocado green – very light
501	blue green – dark
503	blue green – medium
611	drab brown – dark
612	drab brown – medium
640	beige grey – very dark
726	topaz – light
730	olive green – very dark
743	yellow – medium
745	yellow – light pale
809	delft
839	beige brown – dark
840	beige brown – medium
987	forest green – dark
989	forest green
3013	khaki green – light
3052	green grey – medium
3053	green grey
3346	hunter green
3347	yellow green – medium
3348	yellow green – light
3354	dusty rose – light

NEEDLES

Embroidery crewel Nos 7, 8 and 9
Straw or millinery Nos 8 and 9

FABRIC

Size will vary with size of Garland.

Small embroidery hoop 10 cm (4″)
Soft pencil and small embroidery
scissors

APPENDIX D
ALPHABETS

The following are two alphabets that you may like to use when embroidering initials.

$$A \; N \; M \; V \; W \; Z \; Y \; P$$

$$H \; K \; I \; J \; T \; F \; P \; B \; F$$

$$R \; Q \; X \; Y \; U \; S \; L \; F$$

$$G \; C \; E \; O \; D \; A \; V \; Z$$

A B C D E F G

H I J K L M N

O P Q R S T U

V W X Y Z

APPENDIX E
THE FRAMING OF NEEDLEWORK

There are probably as many ways to frame a piece of needlework as there are ways to furnish a room in which the needlework will hang. While most will look attractive, few will be done correctly, and this will be revealed over a period of time.

The most important thing to remember in framing needlework, as indeed in framing any original artwork, is that the nature of the work should not be materially altered during the framing process. In the case of recently completed needlework of the size referred to in this book, this means that, before the embroidery is placed in the frame, it should be laced over archivally sound board in the manner illustrated (see illustration 1). This will keep it firm and straight inside the frame.

It should not be glued down with wet glue or dry mounted in a heat press. Both these methods will cause the fabric to discolour and hasten its deterioration. Neither is it recommended that needlework be stapled on to a backing board or kept in position with masking tape.

Many embroiderers prefer to do the lacing of the work themselves. It is not difficult, merely time-consuming and, therefore, expensive if a professional carries out the operation. Care must be taken to ensure that the weave of the fabric is straight and that the embroidery remains clean. Remember that grease transferred from hands to the surface of the fabric may not show up immediately, but will become apparent in time. Your picture framer should be able to supply you with the correct grade of card on which to lace the embroidery. Having laced the needlework on to its backing, it is ready for framing.

Decisions will now have to be made on what sort of frame best suits the embroidery, whether or not it should be placed behind glass, and if it should be 'matted' with a cardboard surround. These are not only

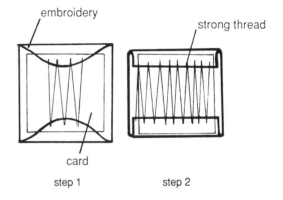

step 1 step 2

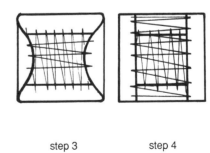

step 3 step 4

Illustration 1: lacing an embroidery — from the back

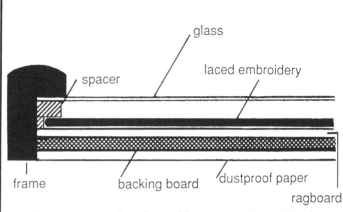

Illustration 2: framing without a matt — side view

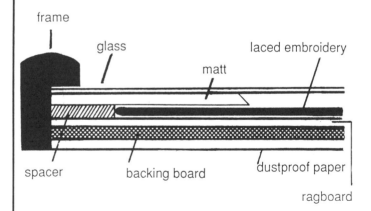

Illustration 3: framing with a matt — side view

aesthetic considerations but also very practical ones.

On cottage embroidery, simple wooden frames, with maybe just a hint of colour along the inside edge, work best. More complicated frames, particularly gilt ones, tend to overwhelm the needlework. Whatever frame is chosen, it should be deep enough and strong enough to accommodate the embroidery, the glass, the backing and any other materials used.

As a general rule, embroideries are best put behind glass. Glazing keeps the dust off, prevents them becoming dirty, and will help keep the silverfish out. However, when the work is glazed, care should be taken that the glass does not touch the surface of the embroidery: moisture condensing on the inside of the glass can migrate into the fabric and cause the fibres to deteriorate. Glass can be kept away from the embroidery either with a small spacer placed between the glass and the embroidery, underneath the rebate of the frame (see illustration 2), or by using a single or double matt (see illustration 3), or a combination of spacer and matt if the surface of the embroidery is raised.

Because the needlework and the glass are separated, non-glare or non-reflective glass should not be used. Most non-glare glass when used in this way blurs the image and dulls the colours. Clear glass is required or, if the embroidery is to hang in a very brightly lit area, a Plexiglas which inhibits the passage of ultra-violet light should be considered.

Except on samplers, matting is recommended as it is not only practical but also serves a very important aesthetic function. An archivally sound, coloured matt (green is often used when the image contains flowers) will not only enhance the image but also prevent the frame from visually crowding the embroidery. Remember that matts look better if they are large – at least five centimetres (2 inches) wide, with the bottom of the matt, slightly larger than the top and the sides, say six or seven centimetres (2½-3 inches). Any smaller than this and the matt and frame may look like concentric, coloured rectangles around the image, and the whole effect will be spoiled.

It is important that the card on which the embroidery is laced, and that used for the matting and backing of the embroidery, is archivally sound. Normal wood-pulp card is not archivally sound. It contains acidic materials which will eventually mark the embroidery.

Finally, when the embroidery is placed in the frame, the frame should be sealed with a good quality tape (not masking tape as it deteriorates too quickly) or completely papered over. This will prevent any dust or insect life entering the frame from the back.

If you adhere to these basic principles this should ensure the long life of the embroidery.

Ross Henty
Canberra Art Framing Company